FEMALE

Christmas

Sing Along with 8 Great-Sounding Tracks

Contents

Page	Title	Full-Performance Track	Sing-Along Track
2	The Gift	1	2
6	Have Yourself a Merry Little Christmas	3	4
10	I'll Be Home for Christmas	5	6
14	It's the Most Wonderful Time of the Year	7	8
18	Let It Snow! Let It Snow! Let It Snow!	9	10
22	Winter Wonderland	11	12
26	Silent Night	15	16
29	O Holy Night (Cantique de Noël)	13	14

Alfred Publishing Co., Inc.
16320 Roscoe Blvd., Suite 100
P.O. Box 10003
Van Nuys, CA 91410-0003
alfred.com

ISBN-10: 0-7390-5601-8 (Book and CD)
ISBN-13: 978-0-7390-5601-1 (Book and CD)

Cover Art:
Microphone © istockphoto.com/picpics

The Gift

Words and Music by
JIM BRICKMAN and TOM DOUGLAS

Verse 1:
Winter snow is falling down,
children laughing all around.
Lights are turning on,
like a fairy tale come true.
Sittin' by the fire we made.
You're the answer when I prayed
I would find someone,
and, baby, I found you.

Chorus:
And all I want is to hold you forever.
And all I need is you more ev'ry day.
You saved my heart from being broken apart.
You gave your love away,
and I'm thankful ev'ry day for the gift.

Verse 2:
Watching as you softly sleep.
What I'd give if I could keep just this moment.
If only time stood still.
But the colors fade away
and the years will make us gray.
But, baby, in my eyes,
you'll still be beautiful.

Chorus:
And all I want is to hold you forever.
All I need is you more ev'ry day.
You saved my heart from being broken apart.
You gave your love away,
and I'm thankful ev'ry day for the gift.

Bridge:
Da da da da da da da. Ooh, hoo, ah.

Chorus:
And all I want is to hold you forever.
All I need is you more ev'ry day.
You saved my heart from being broken apart.
You gave your love away,
I can't find the words to say.
I'm thankful ev'ry day for the gift.

The Gift

Words and Music by
JIM BRICKMAN and TOM DOUGLAS

Have Yourself a
Merry Little Christmas

Words and Music by
HUGH MARTIN and RALPH BLANE

Have yourself a merry little Christmas;
let your heart be light.
From now on, our troubles will be out of sight.

Have yourself a merry little Christmas;
make the Yuletide gay.
From now on, our troubles will be far away.

Here we are as in olden days,
happy golden days of yore.
Faithful friends who are dear to us
gather near to us once more.

Through the years we all will be together,
if the Fates allow.
Hang a shining star upon the highest bough,
and have yourself a merry little Christmas now.

Here we are as in olden days,
happy golden days of yore.
Faithful friends who are dear to us
gather near to us once more.

Through the years we all will be together,
if the Fates allow.
Hang a shining star upon the highest bough,
and have yourself a merry little Christmas now.

And have yourself a merry little Christmas now.

Have Yourself a Merry Little Christmas

Words and Music by
HUGH MARTIN and RALPH BLANE

Slowly (♩ = 76)

Refrain:

Have your-self a mer - ry_____ lit - tle Christ - mas;_____

let your heart be light. From now on, our

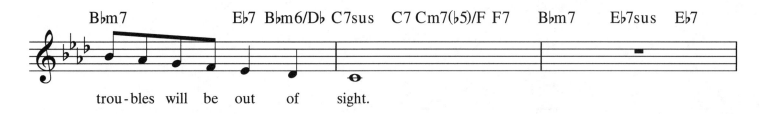

trou-bles will be out of sight.

Have your-self a mer - ry_____ lit - tle Christ - mas;___ make the Yule - tide

gay._____ From now on, our trou-bles will be far a -

Have Yourself a Merry Little Christmas - 3 - 1
31418

8

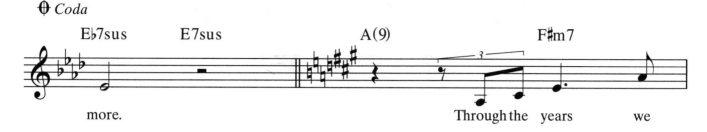

more. Through the years we

all will__ be to-geth - er,___ if the Fates__ al - low.

Hang a shin - ing star up - on the high - est bough,___

___ and have your - self a mer - ry___ lit - tle Christ - mas

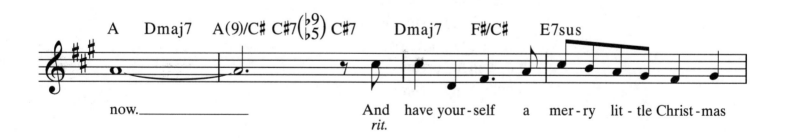

now.___ And have your-self a mer-ry lit - tle Christ-mas
rit.

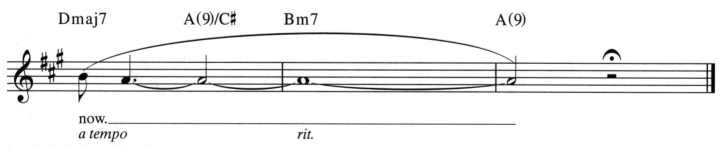

now.___
a tempo   rit.

I'll Be Home for Christmas

Words by
KIM GANNON
Music by
WALTER KENT

Refrain:
I'll be home for Christmas.
You can count on me.
Please have snow and mistletoe
and presents on the tree.

Christmas Eve will find me
where the lovelight gleams.
I'll be home for Christmas,
if only in my dreams.

Verse:
I'm dreaming tonight of a place I know,
even more than I usually do.
And though I know it's a long road back,
I promise you…

Refrain:
I'll be home for Christmas.
You can count on me.

(Instrumental)

Christmas Eve will find me
where the lovelight gleams.
I'll be home for Christmas,
if only in my dreams.
If only in my dreams.

I'll Be Home for Christmas

Words by
KIM GANNON

Music by
WALTER KENT

Moderately slow (♩ = 96)

Refrain:

I'll be home for Christ-mas.

a tempo

You can count on me.

Please have snow and mis-tle-toe and

pres-ents on the tree.

Christ-mas Eve will find me

where the love-light gleams.

I'll Be Home for Christmas - 3 - 1
31418

12

C6   Cm6   G(9)/B   E7sus   E7

I'll   be   home   for   Christ - mas,   if

A13   A7(♯5)   Am7   D7(♭9)   G/D   Gdim7/D   Am7/D

on - ly   in   my   dreams._____

Ddim7   Am7/D   D7(♭9)   Dm7/G   G7   G7(♯5)

A little slower   *rit.*   I'm
Verse:

Cmaj7   Cdim7   G/B   B♭dim7

dream - ing   to - night_____   of   a   place   I   know,___   e - ven

Am7   D7   D7(♯5)   G6   G7(♭9)   G7   Cmaj7   Cdim7

more than   I   u - sual - ly   do.   And   though   I   know   it's   a

G/B   B♭dim7   A9   Am7/D   D7(♭9)

long   road   back,   I   prom - ise   you...
       rit.   *poco accel.*

Refrain:
G6   B♭dim7   Em7/A   D7/A   Em7/A   D7/A   D7

I'll   be   home   for   Christ - mas.
a tempo

G6   Bm7(♭5)   E7   A13   A7(♯5)   A7   A7(♭5)   A7

You   can   count   on   me.

I'll Be Home for Christmas - 3 - 2
31418

I'll Be Home for Christmas - 3 - 3
31418

It's the Most Wonderful Time of the Year

Words and Music by
EDDIE POLA and GEORGE WYLE

It's the most wonderful time of the year.
With the kids jingle-belling
and ev'ryone telling you, "Be of good cheer."
It's the most wonderful time of the year.

It's the hap-happiest season of all.
With those holiday greetings
and gay happy meetings when friends come to call.
It's the hap-happiest season of all.

There'll be parties for hosting,
marshmallows for toasting,
and caroling out in the snow.
There'll be scary ghost stories
and tales of the glories
of Christmases long, long ago.

It's the most wonderful time of the year.
There'll be much mistletoeing
and hearts will be glowing when loved ones are near.
It's the most wonderful time of the year.

(Instrumental)

It's the most wonderful time of the year.
There'll be much mistletoeing
and hearts will be glowing when loved ones are near.
It's the most wonderful time of the year.
It's the most wonderful time of the year.

It's the Most Wonderful Time of the Year

Words and Music by
EDDIE POLA and GEORGE WYLE

It's the Most Wonderful Time of the Year - 3 - 1
31418

16

Emaj7 C♯m7 Bmaj9 G♯m7 C♯m7 F♯7
year.
Bmaj7 Bm7 E7 Amaj7 Dmaj7
Bm7 G♯m7(♭5) E♭7sus E♭7
D.S. 𝄋 al Coda
It's the
𝄌 Coda
B♭m7 E♭7 Fm7 B♭7
time of the year.
A♭/E♭ E♭7sus E♭7
It's the most won - der - ful time of the
A♭maj7/E♭ B♭m7/E♭ A♭maj7/E♭
year.
B♭m7/E♭ A♭maj7/E♭
B♭m7/E♭ A♭maj7

Let It Snow! Let It Snow! Let It Snow!

Words by
SAMMY CAHN
Music by
JULE STYNE

Oh, the weather outside is frightful,
but the fire is so delightful,
and since we've no place to go,
let it snow! Let it snow! Let it snow!

It doesn't show signs of stopping,
and I brought along some corn for popping.
The lights are turned way down low.
Let it snow! Let it snow! Let it snow!

When we finally kiss goodnight,
how I'll hate going out in the storm.
But if you really hold me tight,
say, all the way home I'll be warm.

The fire is slowly dying,
and, my dear, we're still goodbyeing.
But as long as you love me so,
let it snow! Let it snow! Let it snow!

Yeah, as long as you love me so,
I wanna see a lot of snow, uh huh.
Yes, if you love me so,
let it snow! Let it snow! Let it snow!

When we finally kiss goodnight,
how I'll hate going out in the storm.
But if you really hold me tight,
all the way home I'll be warm.

The fire is slowly dying,
and, my dear, we're still goodbyeing.
But as long as you love me so,
let it snow! Let it snow! Let it snow!
let it snow! Let it snow.

Ah, I wanna see a lot of snow,
a lot of lovely, lovely snow.
Let me have a little snow,
snow, snow, a week of snow.

Let It Snow! Let It Snow! Let It Snow!

Words by
SAMMY CAHN

Music by
JULE STYNE

Let It Snow! Let It Snow! Let It Snow! - 3 - 1
31418

fi - nal - ly kiss good - night,___ how I'll hate go - ing out in the storm.___

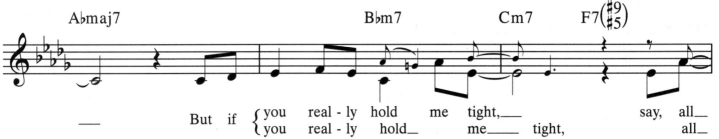

___ But if { you real - ly hold me tight,___ say, all___
{ you real - ly hold___ me___ tight, all___

___ the way home___ I'll___ be warm._____ } The
___ the way home___ I'll be warm.

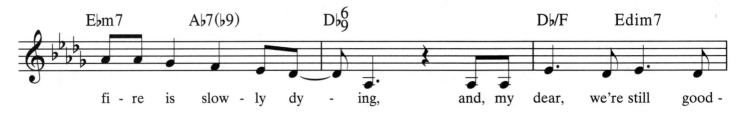

fi - re is slow - ly dy - ing, and, my dear, we're still good -

bye - ing. But as long as you love me so, let it snow!___

Instrumental:

___ Let it snow! Let it snow!

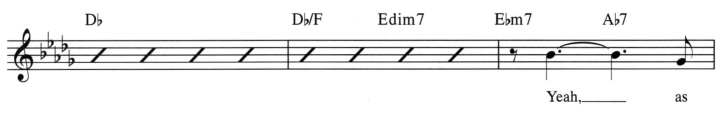

Yeah,_____ as

Winter Wonderland

Words by
DICK SMITH
Music by
FELIX BERNARD

Sleighbells ring, are you list'nin'?
In the lane, snow is glist'nin'.
A beautiful sight, we're happy tonight,
walkin' in a winter wonderland.

Gone away is the bluebird,
here to stay is the new bird.
He sings a love song, as we go along,
walkin' in a winter wonderland!

In the meadow, we can build a snowman,
and pretend that he is Parson Brown.
He'll say, "Are you married?"
We'll say, "No, man!
But you can do the job when you're in town!"

Later on, we'll conspire,
as we dream by the fire,
to face unafraid the plans that we made,
walkin' in a winter wonderland.

In the meadow, we can build a snowman,
and pretend that he's a circus clown.
We'll have lots of fun with Mr. Snowman,
until the other kiddies knock 'em down.

When it snows, ain't it thrillin',
though your nose gets a chillin'?
We'll frolic and play the Eskimo way,
walkin' in a winter wonderland.
To face unafraid the plans that we made,
walking in a winter wonderland.

Winter Wonderland

Words by
DICK SMITH

Music by
FELIX BERNARD

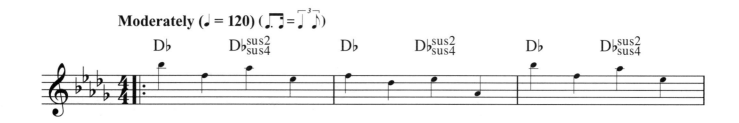

Sleigh - bells ring, are you

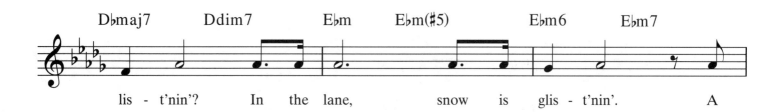

lis - t'nin'? In the lane, snow is glis - t'nin'. A

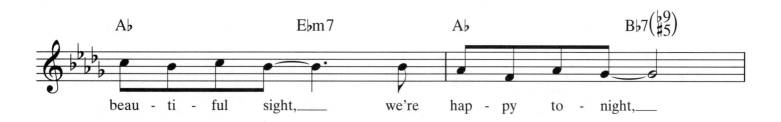

beau - ti - ful sight,____ we're hap - py to - night,____

walk - in' in a win - ter won - der - land. Gone a -

way is the blue - bird, here to stay is the

Winter Wonderland - 3 - 1
31418

Silent Night

Words by
JOSEPH MOHR
Music by
FRANZ GRUBER

Verse 1:
Silent night, holy night,
all is calm, all is bright,
'round yon virgin mother and Child.
Holy Infant, so tender and mild,
sleep in heavenly peace.
Sleep in heavenly peace.

Verse 2:
Silent night, holy night,
shepherds quake at the sight.
Glories stream from heaven afar,
heav'nly hosts sing, "Alleluia.
Christ the Savior is born.
Christ the Savior is born."

Verse 3:
Silent night, holy night,
Son of God, love's pure light.
Radiant beams from Thy holy face,
with the dawn of redeeming grace.
Jesus, Lord at Thy birth.
Jesus, Lord at Thy birth.
Silent night.

Silent Night

Words by
JOSEPH MOHR

Music by
FRANZ GRUBER

Moderately slow (♩ = 92)

mf

Verses 1 & 2:

1. Si - lent night, ho - ly night,
2. Si - lent night, ho - ly night,

all is calm, all is bright,
shep - herds quake at the sight.

'round yon vir - gin moth - er and Child.
Glo - ries stream from heav - en a - far,

Ho - ly In - fant, so ten - der and mild,
heav'n - ly hosts sing, "Al - le - lu - ia.

1.

sleep in heav - en - ly peace.

Sleep in heav - en - ly peace.

Silent Night - 2 - 1
31418

O Holy Night
(Cantique de Noël)

By
ADOLPHE ADAM

O holy night!
The stars are brightly shining,
this is the night of the dear Savior's birth;
long lay the world
in sin and error pining,
till He appeared and the soul felt its worth.

A thrill of hope,
the weary world rejoices,
for yonder breaks
a new and glorious morn!

Fall on your knees!
O hear the angel voices!
O night divine!
O night when Christ was born!
O night, O holy night,
O night divine!

(Repeat from beginning)

O night, O holy night,
O night,
O night divine!

O Holy Night
(Cantique de Noël)

By
ADOLPHE ADAM

*Play 2nd time.